Under the Fig Tree

Visual Prayers and Poems for Lent

ROGER HUTCHISON

Under the Fig Tree

Visual Prayers and Poems for Lent

ROGER HUTCHISON

 Morehouse Publishing
NEW YORK

Unless otherwise noted, the Scripture quotations contained herein are from the New Revised Standard Version Bible, copyright © 1989 by the Division of Christian Education of the National Council of Churches of Christ in the U.S.A. Used by permission. All rights reserved.

Morehouse Publishing, 19 East 34th Street, New York, NY 10016

Morehouse Publishing is an imprint of Church Publishing Incorporated.
www.churchpublishing.org

Cover design by Laurie Klein Westhafer
Typeset by Jennifer Kopec, 2 Pug Design

Library of Congress Cataloging-in-Publication Data

A catalog record of this book is available from the Library of Congress.

ISBN-13: 978-0-8192-3207-6 (pbk.)
ISBN-13: 978-0-8192-3208-3 (ebook)

Printed in Canada

For Kristin

My wife, friend, and
companion on the journey

Contents

Acknowledgments

Fleming Rutledge
My teacher, guide, and friend
Thank you for your encouragement, enthusiasm, and support for this book.
Thank you for the gift of the foreword.
I still have to pinch myself every time I see your name on the cover.

Sharon Ely Pearson
You inspire and teach me.
You met me at The Painting Table and encouraged me to tell the story.
You invited me to bring paints and healing into places that were crying out.
Thank you, once again, for being my editor.
Thank you, always, for being my friend.

The congregation of Trinity Episcopal Cathedral, Columbia, South Carolina
I met you in person on March 9, 1998.
I thank God for the opportunity to have been a part of your family for 6,307 days.
I'll hold you in my heart forever.

The congregation of Palmer Memorial Episcopal Church, Houston, Texas
Thank you for welcoming the Hutchisons with open hearts and outstretched arms.
We are excited about this new chapter in our lives!

Foreword

I t is a special pleasure to write this foreword to Roger Hutchison's newest book, *Under the Fig Tree*. To speak personally for a moment, I confess that I have always had trouble with Lenten disciplines and programs of Scripture reading; it was therefore a happy surprise, a few months ago, to glimpse some of Roger's preliminary drawings and texts. This, I thought, is a biblical journey that I would be glad to take. What you are holding in your hands may look like a children's book, but it has an adult sensibility behind it and asks something of its reader. In this new work, Roger has moved beyond the categories that have previously defined him, producing a volume which invites attention far beyond its deceptively modest appearance.

Anyone who has watched Roger work with children has been struck by his almost magical ability to hold their attention and encourage their participation. He won the lasting affection and gratitude of hundreds of little people and their parents at Trinity Episcopal Cathedral in Columbia, South Carolina, during his remarkable tenure there as Canon for Children's and Family Ministries from 1998 to 2015. Many of those children will remember him all their lives.

When I saw Roger's first book, *The Painting Table*, I was captivated by the richness of color, form, and imagination that characterizes his art and his shaping of it into a narrative. There is a wide-ranging fecundity underlying these images and their context. By providential design, *The Painting Table* was ready to move into a situation its creator never imagined, when the tragic massacre of children in the Sandy Hook Elementary School in Newtown, Connecticut, occurred in 2012.

Newtown's Trinity Episcopal Church invited Roger, bringing his special skills, to minister to the traumatized survivors and their families. There, under his benevolent gaze, the children could work out their distress as the painting table became the image of the Lord's Table where they received communion and the promise of healing. You could almost call it art therapy, but such a term would be reductive. Roger's Christian faith combined with his artistic gifts enlarges his work into a higher realm.

Now, *Under the Fig Tree* appears with its invitation to adults. Above all, it is deeply biblical, which commends it especially to those seeking a closer identification to the Gospel. Roger's seemingly simple sketches catch the eye, but more important, his way of combining biblical texts and pictures gives rise to thought. There is humor, yes, and surprise, but also depth. Passages from the Old and New Testament have inspired his images in a way that brings the participant deeper into the narrative of salvation. It is a joy to commend this lovely book to adults and older children alike.

Fleming Rutledge
Rye Brook, New York
April 21, 2015

Introduction

L ent is a season of the Christian year when people are invited and encouraged to turn their focus on their relationship with God in Christ.

I am a forty-something man. I live a very full and busy life. I pay my bills . . . most of the time. I live in a suburban neighborhood and serve in a place with a lot of people who look just like me. It is a life of GO GO GO . . . all of the time. I have a wife, a daughter, and a "designer dog" that doesn't shed. We drive a Subaru Outback. Subaru's slogan is: "Love. It's what makes a Subaru."

Wow.

All of this got me thinking. What is love . . . really? Of course it is the love I have for God, my family, my friends . . . and okay, our Subaru. Yet . . . as a person of faith, do I really understand love: the bloody, passionate, inspiring, pierced, and challenging face of love? As a forty-something, moving way too quickly through life, do I really know Jesus—the face and heart of love?

Over those past few years, I entered Lent with the fanaticism of someone on a mission—a mission of life and death. I wanted to *know* Jesus in a new way. I wanted to touch his life . . . and walk through his death—and resurrection. I knew that I would glimpse bits and pieces of the story through beautiful liturgies and inspiring Lenten speakers, but I needed more. I needed to be alone with Jesus, and we needed to get to know each other better.

So I began to draw . . . and paint, inspired by different Lenten readings, themes, or stories. I wanted to walk with Jesus—as a friend and disciple. I created a different image each day. These were quick, inspired, and sometimes frantic. I felt at times like a courtroom sketch artist . . . a journalist with paints.

One of my favorite readings—and inspiration for the title of this book—came from John 1:48. Nathanael says to Jesus, "How do you know me?" Jesus replies, with a twinkle in his eye, "I saw you while you were still under the fig tree . . . " I have a special affinity for Nathanael. He understood the importance of making time for prayer. For Jesus to know him and call him by name was profound. Nathanael was, or so he thought, out of sight—hidden. Yet the one that he longed to meet face-to-face not only called Nathanael by name, he also knew Nathanael's heart.

He knows your heart.

Jesus saw Nathanael under the fig tree. I, too, was there. The large green leaves sheltered Nathanael. The ripe fruit-like ornaments hung from the branches. And Jesus saw Nathanael.

I want to be Nathanael.

I think we all want Jesus to see us . . . to call us. And this is where the sparkle in Jesus' eye comes in. He does see us. He does call us. We just need to look up from our computers, our cell phones, our tablets . . . and look out . . . not up. We must look out—into the eyes of Jesus—into the face of Jesus.

How might we gather as a family at the end of the day to read a reflection and explore the meaning of an image? Through conversation and study, I hope this book can be a rich addition to your experience of Lent and will enable you and your family to come to know Jesus' love in a unique and inspiring way.

This book of images and reflections was created with the hope of inspiring others—to slow down. To reflect on what love really means. To sit with Jesus under the fig tree and talk . . . and listen . . . and love.

These are my love letters to Jesus.

Roger Hutchison
Houston, Texas
June 2015

Under the Fig Tree

a_{shes}
      a poignant reminder of the depth of this
season we find ourselves in again

Lent
      we give up and we look up
            we give up and we look in
                  we give up and we look out

up to the face of Christ
in to that intimate place that longs for something more
out to the faces of our brothers and sisters who need
us – and who we need

Lent
remember
may you find comfort and solace in the rhythm of
these holiest of days

'for where your treasure is,
there your heart will be also.'

WEDNESDAY

Remember that you are
dust

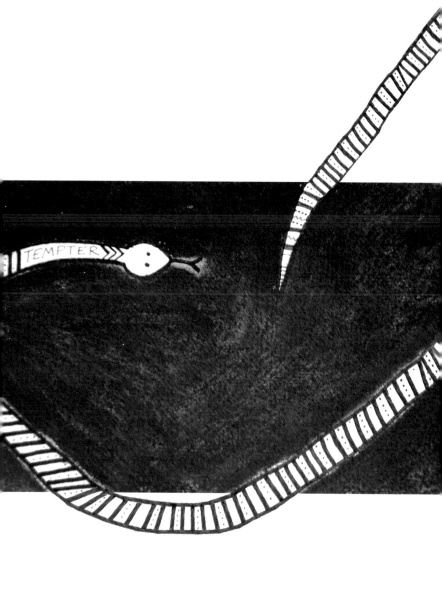

The tempter came and said to him,
"If you are the Son of God, command
these stones to become loaves of bread."

But he answered,
"It is written,
'One does not live by bread alone,
but by every word that comes from
the mouth of God.' "

God spoke the Word incarnate

Jesus
The bread of life

Young wine reveals varying aromas
tastes of fruits and wood
apples, citrus, cherry, plum
vanilla, clove, coconut
with a sharp acidity and the bite of tannin

The young man called Jesus
is new wine

taste and see

New wine into ~~old~~ wineskins.
NEW

h e went to the desert alone
excruciatingly hot days
cold and soulless nights
it was too much
but he stayed

he went to the desert alone
to pray
to listen
to prepare

he was hungry
weary
and
ready

he went to the
desert alone

IN THE DESERT...

turn stones into bread

I'm hungry...

three times he tried to tempt Jesus
three times he failed
"stones to bread"
"throw yourself down Jesus
the angels will save you"
"the kingdom will be yours if you bow
down to me"

when we say Yes
the Word incarnate says
No

I myself did not know him, but the one who
sent me to baptize with water said to me,
"He on whom you see the spirit descend and remain
is the one who baptizes with the Holy Spirit …"

A small child is cradled in his arms
Robed in lace and memories
The people gather 'round and recite the covenant
and water is poured over her head.

"We will with God's help," they say.
The water runs into the child's eyes
and spills onto the floor.

I myself did not know him,
but the one who sent me
to baptize with water said to me, "He on whom you
see the spirit descend and
remain is the one who baptizes with the
Holy Spirit."

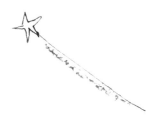

Oh, how I wish I could have been there

waters of baptism
glisten in the holy light
of a descending
dove

God's voice
                    was carried on the *wind*
                                    and the *waves*

"You are my Son,
the Beloved;
with you I am well pleased."

I wish I could have been there

"You are my Son, the Beloved;
with you I am well pleased."

ho are you? Who are you? Who are you? Who are you? Who are you?
e you? Who are you? Who are you? Who are you? Who are you?
ho are you? Who are you? Who are you? who are you? Wh
re you? Who are you? Who are you? Who are you? Wh
re you? Who are you? Who are you? Who are you? Whoo
u? Who are you? Who are you? Who are you? Who are
u? Who are you? Who are you? Who are you? Who are yo
ho are you? Make straight the way of the Lord Who are you?
ho are you? Who are you? Who are you? Who are you? Wh
re you? Who are you? Who are you? Who are you? Who are
ou? Who are you? I who AM are THE you? ONE who a
ou? Who are you? Who are you? who are you? Who are you.
ho are you? Who are you? Who are you? Who are you? W
re you? who are you? RYING who are out I who are you
ho are you? Who are you? Who are you? Who are you? Who
re you? Who are you? Who are you? Who are you? Who ar
u? Who are you? IN who THE are WI you DERNES
ho are you? Who are you? Who are you? Who are you?
ho are you? Who are you? Who are you? Who are you? Who are you

There have been many
who have given voice to the voiceless.
Many who have cried out in the wilderness.

Martin Luther King Jr. cried out for justice
and equality.
He marched and preached and loved.
Then a bullet silenced his voice.
But it silenced not a nation.
Or did it?

John the Baptist cried out, "I am the voice of one
crying out in the wilderness,
'Make straight the way of the Lord,'" as the prophet
Isaiah said.

The hands of the carpenter
Rough and calloused
Cradle the newborn child.

"Why?" He wonders.
"I am but a poor carpenter.
And Mary, just a young girl."

"Protect and love this child."
Joseph remembers the
words of the angel.

He adjusts the blanket snugly around his son
And pulls him close to his chest.

The animals' jet black eyes watch from the shadows
of the stable.

The stars twinkle in the night sky.

Mary sleeps.

Joseph whispers . . . "I love you, my son."

Joseph loved Jesus.

"Jesus was about thirty years old when he
began his work. He was the son of Joseph"

Nathanael asked him, "Where did you come to know me?"

Jesus answered, "I saw you under the fig tree."

Nathanael replied, "Rabbi, you are the Son of God! You are the King of Israel!"

Jesus answer, "You will see greater things than these."

Large leaves cast shadows on the ground.
The fruit sweet with sunshine and promise hung like ornaments
from the branches.

Nathanael went to shade of the fig tree to pray.

Philip, with a palpable intensity and joy, called out to him
"Come and see! We found him! He's the one whom Moses and the
prophets wrote about. Jesus the son of Joseph from Nazareth."

He had his doubts.

"What good can come from Nazareth?"

"Come and see!" Philip cried out again.

Reluctantly, he left the shade of the fig tree
and followed Philip.

When Jesus saw the men approaching, he called out to Nathanael,
"Here is truly an Israelite in whom there is no deceit!"

Nathanael stopped in his tracks.

He gazed into the man's face. "How did you know me?"
He wondered if Philip had told him who he was.

With a twinkle in his eye, the man called Jesus answered,
"I saw you under the fig tree."

After a lifetime of seeking and prayer, Nathanael knew that this
indeed was the Son of God."

The leaves of the fig tree danced with joy in the breeze.

As he was walking along, he saw Levi, Son of Alphaeus, sitting at the tax booth, and he said to him . . .

follow me

✝✝✝

I wonder how I would respond?

And he got up and followed him.

${\rm T}$wo simple words.

"Follow me."

He called the tax collector by name.
"Levi."

"Follow me."

Levi, without hesitation, got up, left everything behind, and followed him.

Oh . . . may I have the faith of Levi.

Jesus traveled through all the cities and villages
teaching

      proclaiming

           healing

The sick and the lonely
touched his robes
The lame cried out his name
The crowds grew

              seeking sustenance

              craving each and every word

"Come near," he said.
"I have some Good News to share with you."

Jesus traveled about from one town and
village to the next proclaiming the good
news of the Kingdom of God.

He drew a ⊂×⊃ in the sand

I wonder.

Who are you?

You look different than me.

I am afraid.

Your clothes are torn and tattered.

I want to turn away.

You speak in a language different than mine.

I am confused.

I want to turn my back on you.

But I remain.

Your eyes – they captivate me.

They pull me in and I begin to

sense a connection.

You bend down and make your mark in the sand.

I bend down and make my mark in the sand.

The lines intersect.

We are drawn together by a fish – a symbol of the One

who calls us by name.

I tell you my name.

You tell me yours.

We are family.

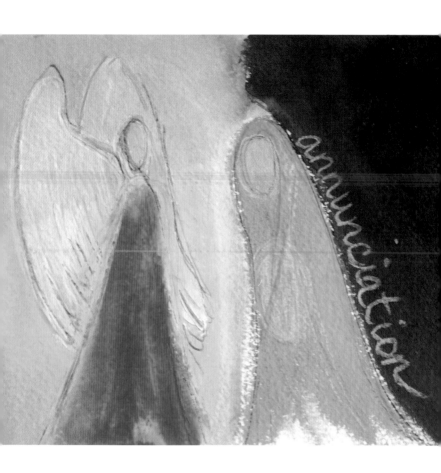

annunciation

What a day this has been!
I didn't hear him knock on the door.
I didn't hear the neighborhood dogs barking.
He was just there.
                    Like the wind.
"Do not be afraid," he said.
"You are going to have a son."
"His name will be Jesus."

I am going to have a baby.
A baby boy and his name will be Jesus.
I wonder…
Why me?

I am blind to
injustice
racism
discrimination
oppression
inequity
inequality
corruption
        Jesus!
                Please help me to see!

"Once more Jesus put his hands on the man's eyes.
Then his eyes were opened, his sight was restored,
and he saw everything clearly."

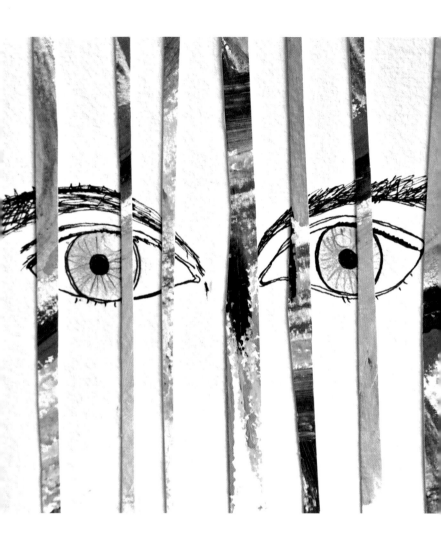

Companion – "with bread"

The hungry cry out

for justice

  for peace

    for healing

      for shelter

        for touch

          for friendship

            for community

            for equality

              for purpose

              for safety

for *love*

Jesus says "I am the bread of life."

Take and eat.

Be my companion.

Share with others.

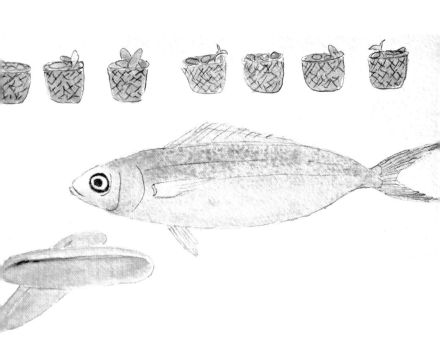

loaves and fishes

never
lose hope.

Winter branches
shudder and *shiver* in the brittle cold.

It is quiet.
The gray clouds
heavy with sadness and loss
sulk across the sky.

Remember.
Remember.
Remember.

Three days.
Just beneath the surface.
Hope abides.
New life is coming…

Gathered around a still pool of water
the sheep drink their fill.
The place they have gathered is surrounded
by open fields and high cliffs.

The place they have gathered is a dangerous place.
They are not afraid.
The shepherd watches her flock.
The shepherd protects her flock.
The shepherd calls each sheep by name.
The shepherd leads her flock.

My sheep listen to my voice; I know them, and they
follow me.

John 10:27

"This little light of mine
I'm going to let it shine."
But what if I can't?
What if I don't?

The light flickers dimly
                threatening to go out.
There are days when the lamp will not burn
Moments when my faith is weak

Then out of the darkness

a still small voice whispers my name.

"Be ready."
"Tend to your soul."
"Make sure your lamp is filled."
"I will return."
"Let your light shine."
                "Be ready."

Make sure you have enough oil for your lamp.
"I'm coming to meet you again."

I am the vine

I remember

Swinging from the vine in the woods behind my childhood home.

Summer joy

Free falling.

Boyhood games.

Holding on for dear life.

Letting go and crashing to the ground

I am grown now and have little time for childhood games.

My hands still remember the rough bark in my young hands.

The vine dropping down from a place so high that I could not see where
it began

Did it drop from the sky?

Was it from Heaven?

Yes.

It was.

Incarnate.

"I am the vine."

Hold on for dear life.

*W*e've been given a mind.
Open it.

We've been given a heart.
Love one another.

We've been given a voice.
Tell the truth.

We've been given ears.
Listen before you speak.

We've been given eyes.

Look beneath the surface.

We've been given feet and hands.
Go in peace to love and serve.

We've been given much.
Share it with one another.

"Give your talents to the others.
You did not use what I gave you.
I will not give you anymore."

abide in me

R_{est}

in me.

Remain

in me.

Abide

in me.

Be not afraid.

I will never leave you.

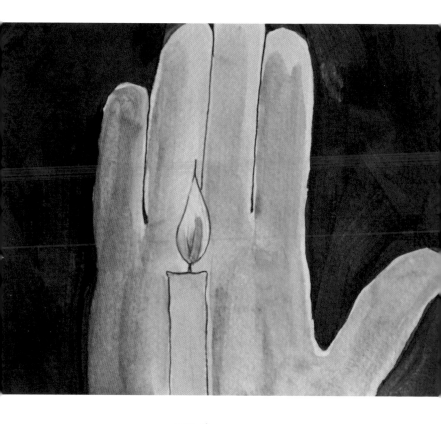

Sleeper awake!

Fear and anxiety has a way of *creeping* in especially in the **dark** of night.

Am I good enough?

Have I done enough?

Am I of any value?

Why am I here?

Then morning comes

and the light pours through the window.

My sleepy and swollen eyes open . . . tentatively at first.

Morning has come.

Sleeper awake!

Christ shines upon me!

"Strike the rock
and water will come out."
Moses listened and did as God said.
The water poured forth.
The place was called Massah and Meribah.

Years passed
And the well that supplied the Israelites with water
dried up.
God instructed Moses
Command the rock to produce water.

Moses did not listen to God and struck the
rock twice.
Water poured forth
as did the wrath of God.
The one whose name means
"from the waters he was drawn"
was unable to bring the people into the land that God
has provided them.
A life of deep hardship
came upon them.

Strike the rock and
water will come out.

God the
    Father
    Mother
    Creator
    Sustainer

God the
    Son
    Teacher
    Crucified
    Resurrected

God the
    Holy Spirit
    Flame
    Ghost
    Comforter

Three in one
                    No beginning
                                No end

Friends (and the betrayer)
Gathered around the table
To share
Wine and olives
Bread and fish
Jesus
begins to speak
Hearts
began to break…
Eucharist

in remembrance of me.

I will soon be leaving you
He reached for the cup
My blood
Do this.
Remember me.
The bread, then held aloft.
Remember me.
Body broken
Bread of Heaven

Christ our Passover is sacrificed for us.

I. I do not know him.
   II. I do not know him.
      III. I do not know him.

The cock crowed

Peter the rock
met eyes with Jesus
And he knew that what Jesus had said
was true

Peter ran away
        Weeping

Even after his betrayal Jesus never stopped *loving*
Peter.

Weary and lonely
He retreated to the garden to pray.
Broken
Human
and divine
Collapsed to the ground

God!

I cannot do this

Please!

If it is your will
Remove this cup from me
Anguished and pleading
His sweat
Became like great drops of
Blood
Falling to the ground

They spit on him

Mocked him

They struck his head

Blinding pain

All dignity gone

They stripped away his clothing

Bruised and battered

They led him away

Jesus
Receives his cross
His mind wanders to when he was a child
in his father's carpentry shop
 smooth wood and sawdust
 tables and chairs
The wood of the cross is not smooth
It is rough
It is heavy
 It is
 where he will die
As a criminal

On the road

Jesus sees his mother

Mary

Her eyes wide

With fear and anguish

She is his mother and her heart is shattering

But she knows

This is his destiny

Her destiny

She wants to *rush in* and hold him

Tend to his wounds

She stands firm - a pillar of silence and love

She watches him as he turns his face toward

Calgary

Close your eyes
And see the face of Christ.
Eyes filled with love
And determination
Sadness and longing
Touch his bruised cheek
Like Veronica, wipe away the sweat and blood
Care for him,
Be present with him.
Serve him.

Open your eyes
And see the face of Christ in your neighbor.
Take her hand and walk with her
Share your food and drink so that she is not
hungry or thirsty
Protect her from danger.
Care for her.
Be present with her.
Serve her.

The women gathered
On the side of the road so they could see Jesus.
Weeping and wailing
They reached out to him as he approached.

"Do not weep for me!" he cried out.
Weep for yourselves.
Weep for your children.

The day of judgment is near.

The stars *twinkle* and *shine*
In the ink-stained night sky
She stands at the base of the
Winter tree
Branches bare and outstretched
She grieves for what has been lost
She longs for what is to be
She remembers his words.

At the base of the tree
A flower appears.
New life is coming.

The end is near.
He cries out with a loud voice…

Why?

Why have you forsaken me?

I'm standing in the crowd below
And I can see the pain in Jesus' face
I wonder what he is saying.
I wonder who he is calling.
Someone says he is calling Elijah.

The skies begin to darken.
A hush falls over the crowd.

I forgive you.
He says to the criminal.
He prays for his mother.
He prays for his friends.
There
In agony
He gives his all

With one last painful breath
Jesus dies.

Jesus cried with a loud voice!

My God, my God, why have you forsaken me?

Eli, Eli, lema sabachthani . . . and he breathed his last . .

75

Passion
Beautiful and **painful love**
A journey like
No other.
Let me walk with you Jesus.
Let me hold your cross when it gets too heavy.
I wish I could save you.

      But I can't.

      It hurts me to see you this way.

My shepherd
My friend
My Lord

Holy love
Generous love
Ultimate love

In giving
His all
Jesus
Gave us
Eternal life
We receive your
Gift
with praise and thanksgiving
Eternal gratitude
Redemption

pas•sion
/paSHən/

1. strong and barely controllable emotion
2. the suffering and death of Jesus

Latin . pati . suffer   .INRI.

We adore you O Christ,
and we bless you

Because by your holy cross
you have redeemed the world

It is
finished.

Tetelestai

He bowed his head and
Released his spirit

The cross
Stands in silence
On a hill
Golgotha
The place of the skull
Death has come

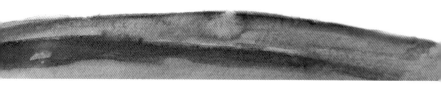

Once the crowd dispersed
Two friends remained
With permission,
They removed his body from the cross

Gently

Tenderly

They covered his broken body with myrrh and aloe
They wrapped him
In strips of linen
They brought him to a garden
Where there was
a tomb

Jesus, now you can
feel no pain.
No hateful
statements or lies
can wound you.
Soldiers pull out
the spikes and release
your body from
the cross.

86   Under the Fig Tree

The winter soil
Cold and damp
Holds a promise
Deep roots
Seek nourishment
And light

Into the tomb
They place his body.
His body
A promise
Is growing

I grieve.
I wander around in a fog
Of emotion
and fear

The one I love
Is no more
I saw it with my own eyes
He is gone
I see his face in my dreams
He is not there when I awake
There is no peace

I wonder if I can go on.

Early in the morning
Mary Magdalene
Went to the tomb
    Her head began to spin
    Something was awry!
The stone
    Rolled away
His body
    Gone!

She turned away not knowing where to go
The gardener was there.
"Where is he?" she cried.
He said to her, "Mary."
She turned and saw
His face in a new light
"Rabboni!" she cried!

91

The journey has brought you
Here.
　　　To this place.

The tomb
His body waits.

We are his body now.
He calls us to go.
　　　He calls us to seek and serve.

He calls us to love.
He calls us to be his light in the world.

At times
We feel alone.
At times
The challenge is too much.
But we keep walking.
We keep moving.
We are not alone.
　　We will never be alone.

The colors of passion
Spread out across the canvas
My fingers—active participants in the story
  Begin to move the colors
  A chaotic and stirring dance
  born from the depth of my artist's soul.

Darkness becomes light
The horizon
A thin place
Between heaven and earth

The tomb is empty
And the sun shines
With a holy fire
Sending streaks of vibrant and shimmering
light across the sky
  I can feel my heart beating in my chest!

The colors fill the canvas and spill over the edge and
onto The Painting Table.
My hands open wide
Covered with the colors of God's forgiving love.
I raise them to the sky!
Alleluia! Alleluia! Alleluia!
Christ is risen today!!!

About the Paintings and Reflections

I approach painting as a form of prayer. I sit at my painting table for a while in silence—listening for that "still small voice." I then begin to select my colors and enter into the process of translating my prayers into paintings. I never know what the outcome will be. During Lent one year, I read a piece of scripture daily and prayed. I wrote as well as painted, using a variety of media. With *Under the Fig Tree: Visual Prayers and Poems for Lent* I share my results.

1. Charcoal on Paper, *Isaiah 58:1-12*
2. Charcoal on Paper, *Matthew 4:1-11*
3. Charcoal and Colored Pencil on Paper, *Luke 5:36-39*
4. Charcoal on Paper, *Luke 5:16*
5. Charcoal and Sharpie on Paper, *Matthew 4:3*
6. Watercolor and Ink Pen on Paper, *Mark 1:8*
7. Ink Pen and Oil Pastels on Paper, *Luke 3:22*
8. Ink Pen on Paper, *John 1:23*
9. Ink Pen and Sharpie on Paper, *Matthew 1:18-25*
10. Watercolor and Pencil on Paper, *John 1:43-51*
11. Ink Pen and Sharpie on Paper, *Mark 2:14*
12. Watercolor and Pencil on Paper, *Matthew 9:35*
13. Oil Pastel on Paper, *John 8:1-11*
14. Oil Pastel on Paper, *Luke 1:31*
15. Watercolor, Ink Pen, and Mixed Media on Paper, *Mark 8:22-25*
16. Watercolor and Pencil on Paper, *John 6:35*

17. Sharpie and Marker on Paper, *Matthew 12:40*
18. Watercolor and Pencil on Paper, *John 10:27*
19. Watercolor and Pencil on Paper, *Matthew 25:1-13*
20. Watercolor and Pencil on Paper, *John 15:5*
21. Sharpie, Ink Pen, and Watercolor on Paper, *Matthew 25:14-30*
22. Sharpie and Watercolor on Paper, *John 15:4*
23. Ink Pen and Watercolor on Paper, *Ephesians 5:14*
24. Acrylic, Oil Pastel, and Pencil on Paper, *Numbers 20:8-12*
25. Acrylic on Canvas, *Matthew 28:19*
26. Acrylic on Canvas, *Luke 22:7-38*
27. Watercolor and Pencil on Paper, *Mark 14:12-26*
28. Watercolor and Pencil on Paper, *Luke 22:59-62*
29. Acrylic on Canvas, *Luke 22:39-46*
30. Acrylic and Pencil on Paper, *Matthew 26:67*
31. Acrylic on Paper, *John 19:17*
32. Acrylic on Paper, *John 19:26-27*
33. Acrylic on Paper, *Isaiah 53:2-3 and Psalm 27:8-9*
34. Acrylic on Paper, *Luke 23:27-31*
35. Acrylic on Canvas Board, *John 19:25*
36. Ink Pen and Watercolor on Paper, *Matthew 27:46*
37. Acrylic and Oil Pastel on Canvas Board, *Matthew 27:50*
38. Acrylic on Paper, *Mark 15:21*
39. Watercolor and Ink Pen on Paper, *2 Corinthians 9:15*
40. Acrylic on Paper, *John 19:30*
41. Acrylic on Paper, *Mark 15:22*
42. Acrylic and Oil Pastel on Paper, *John 19:38*
43. Acrylic on Paper, *Matthew 27:60*
44. Acrylic on Canvas Board, *Luke 24:13*
45. Acrylic on Paper, *John 20:1*
46. Acrylic on Paper, *Mark 16:19-20*
47. Acrylic on Paper, *John 20:18*